A QUICK GUIDE TO FILM DIRECTING

A QUICK GUIDE TO FILM DIRECTING

RAY MORTON

AN IMPRINT OF HAL LEONARD CORPORATION

Published in 2014 by Limelight Editions

An Imprint of Hal Leonard Corporation

7777 West Bluemound Road

Milwaukee, WI 53213

Trade Book Division Editorial Offices

33 Plymouth St., Montclair, NJ 07042

Printed in the United States of America

Book design by Mark Lerner

Library of Congress Cataloging-in-Publication Data

Morton, Ray, 1961-
 A quick guide to film directing / Ray Morton.
    pages cm
 ISBN 978-0-87910-806-9 (pbk.)
 1. Motion pictures--Production and direction. I. Title.
 PN1995.9.P7M585 2014
 791.4302'33--dc23

                           2014008765

www.limelighteditions.com

For Erin, Jack, and Sean Morton
and
Caitlin Hoey
and
Aiden James Masterbone

Contents

Introduction

The director is the pivotal figure in the creation of a motion picture.

It takes an army of talented people to make a movie, but it takes a director to lead that army. The director devises the overall creative concept for the production, hires the cast and key members of the creative team, sets the tone and calls the shots on the set and in the editing room, and has final say in all creative matters affecting the film.

The contributions of everyone working on a movie—the producer, the screenwriter, the cinematographer, the editor, the production and costume designers, the composer, the technical crew, and the actors—are all filtered through the director's concept, judgment, and taste to create the final cinematic work.

Directing a film requires a unique combination of artistic vision, technical expertise, and managerial skill. This book will provide you with a comprehensive look at the essential talents and tasks required to successfully helm a motion picture.

CHAPTER 1

A Brief History of Film Directing

The job of film directing was born with the cinema itself.

The first movies were short documentaries—brief clips of real-life situations such as a train pulling into a station, workers leaving a factory, a man sneezing, and so on. These scenes were filmed by the various men around the globe who invented the movie camera—men such as Louis Le Prince and William Friese-Greene in England, Louis and Auguste Lumière in France, and William Kennedy Laurie Dickson in the United States. These inventors figured out how to transform still cameras capable of recording only one static image at a time into machines that could record (on a strip of flexible celluloid) a series of images in rapid succession that, when projected back at the same rate at which they were shot, could create the illusion of a picture that moved. Initially, the Lumières, Dickson, and their fellow innovators created their moving images by simply setting up their cameras and recording whatever happened in front of them. Before long, however, the men began choosing their subjects more deliberately. As they made their decisions about what subjects to photograph, where to place the camera, and when to begin and end the recording, these technicians inadvertently became film directors.

The cameras created by these inventors were soon acquired by others—businesspeople, showmen, and artists—who began to make movies for public consumption, and thus, the film industry was born. Audiences soon grew tired of documentary scenes, and so moviemakers began using their cameras to tell fictional stories—comedies, dramas, romances, and action spectaculars—in the form of five-, ten-, and twenty-minute shorts. The director was the key figure in this process.

Early movie directors were total filmmakers—they would usually dream up and write the scenarios, organize and run the production, help build the sets and find the locations, cast the actors and tell them what to do, photograph the scenes, create the special and visual effects, and edit the results. In the process, directors such as Edwin S. Porter and D. W. Griffith began to pioneer the various techniques—close-ups, intercutting, and so on—that would become the foundation of the "language" of film.

As movies grew longer—eventually into ninety-plus-minute features—and more complex, and the production process became more involved, individual specialists (screenwriters, cinematographers, art directors, editors, and so on) began to assume responsibility for the various tasks required to make a movie, leaving directors to function more as a creative overseers than as hands-on functionaries. Directors remained, however, the primary artistic drivers of the filmmaking process.

For American directors, this began to change with the rise of the studio system in the 1920s. During the approximately thirty-year-long studio era, company-designated producers working for a strong production chief became the prime movers of individual film projects—the producers found the properties, hired the writers, and developed the stories and scripts. They also cast the films, selected the key members of the creative team, and supervised the production process. Directors, most of whom were under long-term contract to the studio, became hired hands—important ones, to be sure, but still subservient to producers. Directors in this era usually did not participate in the creative development of a project, but instead were simply assigned to a particular film a few days before shooting began and then reassigned to another project as soon as the picture wrapped. The producer would oversee the editing and completion of the final product.

Studio-era directors had little or no say in what pictures they were assigned to, and it was not unusual for several directors to be put to work on a single movie; if a director fell ill, or a producer was unhappy with his work, or the director was unavailable for reshoots because he was working on another project, then another helmer (a nickname for director coined by the show-business trade paper *Variety*) would be assigned to take over. While some higher-profile directors such as Frank Capra, John Ford, and Howard Hawks had more control over their work than their brethren, even they had to operate under relatively tight constraints.

As the studio system came to an end in the 1950s and early 1960s, most directors who were formally under contract went freelance, moving from one studio to another as they took on different projects. This samurai status gave helmers who made pictures that were successful at the box office more clout, allowing them to choose the projects they wanted to do and to negotiate greater creative input and freedom from the producers and companies who were eager to hire them.

During this period, American directors also began to gain more critical respect. This was due in large part to the influence of *la politique des Auteurs*, a.k.a. "the auteur theory," a critical perspective devised by a group of French movie critics (led by future directors François Truffaut and Jean-Luc Godard) writing for the respected film journal *Cahiers du Cinéma* and later popularized in the United States by critic Andrew Sarris. The theory saw directors as the primary creative *auteurs* (authors) of the films they made, and as a consequence of it, movie directors in the U.S. began to be regarded by critics, viewers, studio executives, and themselves not just as competent technicians (the prevailing view for most of the studio era), but also as legitimate visionary artists.

This view was bolstered by the increased distribution and popularity in America of foreign films—movies from England, France, Sweden, and other countries where directors had retained their creative clout over the years and were definitely the artistic authors of their movies—as well as by the beginning of an independent film movement in the U.S. that saw young directors who very much considered themselves auteurs making personal films that reflected their own unique creative ideas and artistic points of view.

All this approbation came to a head in the late 1960s and early 1970s, when the incredible success of innovative films such as *Bonnie and Clyde*, *The Graduate*, *Easy Rider*, *The Last Picture Show*, *The Godfather*, *The Exorcist*, *American Graffiti*, and *Jaws* turned their directors (Arthur Penn, Mike Nichols, Dennis Hopper, Peter Bogdanovich, Francis Ford Coppola, William Friedkin, George Lucas, and Steven Spielberg) into superstars.

The 1970s became the Decade of the Director: during this period, movie helmers became celebrities as well known, lauded, and sought after as the star actors who appeared in their movies. Directors were taken seriously as creative artists and were regarded as significant cultural figures and commentators by the intelligentsia, by academia, and by the general public. Most important, directors were given almost unlimited creative freedom and control over their projects by producers and studios—conditions that led to what many consider a golden age in American and world filmmaking.

Unfortunately, all that freedom also led to financial and artistic self-indulgence on the part of many directors, which resulted in a string of big-budget flops in the latter half of the 1970s. When the creative and box-office failure of Michael Cimino's wildly over-budget western epic *Heaven's Gate* brought about the collapse of United Artists (the company that financed the film) in 1980, other studios began to take back the control they had ceded to directors over the previous fifteen or so years.

Throughout the 1980s and 1990s, studios tightened their grips on project selection and development, as well as on budgets and finances. The director was still seen as the key creative figure in the making of a film, and successful helmers still had a great deal of latitude in making their pictures, but nowhere near the unfettered free rein they'd enjoyed in the 1970s. Filmmakers in this era had more freedom in the independent movement, which thrived throughout the 1980s and 1990s and continued to afford enterprising auteurs the opportunity to create unique personal films, as long as they could do so on reasonably modest budgets.

The modern era is presenting film directors with a great many challenges. The big studios are making fewer movies on a narrower range of subjects and exercising greater and greater control over the productions. At the same time, the independent theatrical market has all but evaporated. All these developments leave helmers with fewer opportunities and outlets to ply their trade in traditional fashion. On the bright side, new technologies such as digital motion picture cameras and editing programs for home computers are making it easier for directors to make movies outside of the conventional arenas, and new release platforms (including Internet-based distribution through venues such as You-Tube, iTunes, and the various streaming services, as well as cable-television-based options such video-on-demand) provide numerous new ways to deliver films to receptive viewers.

So, while forms and formats may be changing, the need and desire to tell stories on film persist, which means that people are going to go on directing movies for a long time to come.

CHAPTER 2

How to Become a Film Director

There are many paths one can take to become a film director:

Make an interesting short

Films students in undergraduate and graduate programs and independents working on their own who make striking short films frequently attract the attention of agents, managers, producers, and studio executives, who may offer them opportunities.

Direct in other media

Directors who do notable work in other arenas—television, theater, commercials, or music videos—are often recruited to make feature films.

Come up through the ranks

People who do well in other areas of filmmaking—producers, screenwriters, actors, editors, cinematographers, and even stunt coordinators—can sometimes leverage their success into opportunities to direct.

Just do it

Some people become directors by making their own movies from scratch. These folks write their own scripts, raise the money to make the films, and then go out and shoot them.

CHAPTER 3

A Few Things a Film Director Should Know

A film director's primary function is to tell a story on the big screen. To do this successfully, he must have a working knowledge of the following:

1. Dramatic storytelling

Movie storytelling is dramatic storytelling—the presentation of a narrative in which a protagonist in pursuit of a significant goal becomes involved in a conflict that leads to climax, resolution, and ultimately transformation—so a director must have a basic understanding of dramatic structure. Dramatic structure is the template based on the core principles of dramatic writing first set down by Aristotle in ancient Greece and refined by dramatists across the millennia; it contains all the key elements of dramatic storytelling: exposition, rising action, suspense, surprise, reversal, climax, falling action, and denouement. According to this template, a dramatic narrative is divided into three sections called *acts*, which unfold as follows:

ACT I

- The world in which the story takes place is introduced.
- The Protagonist is introduced and his circumstances are laid out.
- Key supporting characters, the relationships between the characters, and additional important story elements are also established.
- A crucial event occurs that sets the story in motion. This event is called the *inciting incident*.
- At the end of Act I, something happens that changes the Protagonist's situation in some very drastic way. This event is called the *catalyst*. It is also known at the first plot point, the first turning point, the first plot twist, the Act I plot twist, or the complication.
- As a result of this catalyst, the Protagonist develops a significant goal he becomes determined to achieve. That goal can be big (to save the world) or small (to save a local landmark); it can be internal (to overcome a trauma) or external (to find a buried treasure); it can be personal (to find love) or public (to stop global warming).

ACT II

- The Protagonist—usually working against some sort of tension-generating, "ticking clock" deadline—develops a plan for accomplishing his goal and then sets out to follow it.

- The Protagonist's quest to achieve his objective brings him into contact with the Antagonist, who is or becomes determined to stop the Protagonist from accomplishing his goal.
- During his quest, the Protagonist encounters a series of obstacles—primarily generated by the Antagonist—that stand between him and his objective.
- The Protagonist usually begins Act II at a disadvantage (thanks to the catalyst), but uses his inner and outer resources—which can include special skills and abilities and help from unusual allies—to overcome these obstacles (which become bigger, more complex, and more difficult to deal with as the narrative progresses) and begins to march toward victory.
- Near the end of Act II, the Protagonist closes in on that victory. He reaches a point where it appears that he is about to achieve his goal. Success seems to be within his grasp.
- At this point, something happens that once again drastically changes the Protagonist's circumstances. This event—usually instigated by the Antagonist— robs the Protagonist of his impending triumph and leaves him in a defeated (and often precarious) position, facing an obstacle so formidable that it appears he will never be able to overcome it and, as a result, will fail to ever accomplish his goal. This event is known as the *catastrophe*. It is also known at the second plot point, the second turning point,

the second plot twist, the Act II plot twist, the second complication, or the crash-and-burn.

ACT III

- As Act III begins, all hope appears to be lost. The Protagonist has been defeated and it seems as though he will never be able to achieve his objective.

- At this point—when the Protagonist is at his absolute lowest—something happens that allows him or motivates him to rally.

- The Protagonist now does one of two things: he either comes up with a new plan to achieve his original objective, or he abandons that objective and comes up with an entirely new goal (and a plan to achieve it).

- The Protagonist sets out to put his new plan into action.

- This leads to the story's *climax*: a final confrontation with the Antagonist in which the Protagonist is finally able to overcome the seemingly insurmountable obstacle—usually by defeating the Antagonist—and accomplish his goal (or not, if that's what the story calls for).

- Act III concludes with the *resolution*, which shows how all the story's problems are resolved and how things work out for all the characters as a result of the climax. The resolution often indicates how things are expected to go for the characters after the story ends.

- A key function of the resolution is to show how the Protagonist has changed. At its core, drama is about transformation,
and the Protagonist of a dramatic tale always undergoes a
profound change as a result of his experiences in the story.
This change is usually for the better—the Protagonist solves
a personal problem, repairs a broken relationship, learns
an important life lesson, achieves fame and fortune, etc.—
although sometimes it can be for the worse—e.g., a good
cop becomes corrupt; an idealistic woman becomes cynical;
a sane man descends into madness. This transformation is
often called the Protagonist's "arc."

A director needs to understand dramatic structure so he
can analyze the story he is telling and devise the imagery,
action, staging, and cutting that will highlight, emphasize,
and communicate the key narrative elements to viewers, so
they can clearly comprehend the tale.

2. Genre conventions and clichés

Most film stories are genre stories. Major movie genres include: Action; Adventure; Thriller (Crime, Caper, Psycho-
logical); Comedy (Romantic, Screwball, Buddy, Underdog;
Spoof); Drama (Social Issue, Courtroom, Medical, Family); Mystery; Horror (Monster, Supernatural, Slasher); Sci-
ence Fiction; Fantasy; Western; Sports (Comedy or Drama);
and Biopic. Every genre has certain specific narrative and

structural elements and conventions that must be included in a movie's plot for that movie to be considered part of that genre. For example:

- Romantic Comedies must have a "cute meet"—a scene in which the two leads first encounter each other in some quirky or amusing fashion. The leads must take an immediate dislike to one another. Later they must overcome that dislike in a sequence in which the pair is forced to be together under trying circumstances, at which point they warm to one another and eventually fall in love. There must then be a silly misunderstanding that causes the two leads to break up at the end of Act II, and they must get back together at the end of Act III.

- Sports movies always feature an underdog player or team no one thinks can win; an unconventional coach who is the only person who believes in the player or the team; a rival player or team that appears to outmatch the underdog in every way; a training sequence in which the underdog player or team gets up to speed; and, of course, a final game or match in which the underdog takes a terrible beating before coming from behind, against all odds, to win.

- Fantasy films usually present a callow young hero who receives a call to adventure that he first rejects, and then later accepts; a mentor who informs the hero that he possesses some sort of amazing power and then teaches him to use it; a villain with powers that rival the hero's; a beautiful young woman for the hero to rescue and romance; and a final battle in which the forces of good clash with and eventually triumph over the forces of evil.

- Mysteries always have a crime (usually a murder), a red herring (a character that appears to be guilty of committing the crime but eventually turns out to be innocent), and a "revealing the true culprit" scene; Courtroom Dramas always climax with a big trial; Thrillers and Action movies usually feature car chases, fistfights and gunfights, and a valuable MacGuffin (an object everyone is searching for or fighting over); and so on.

When making a genre story, a director must incorporate these elements and conventions into the film in some fashion so as not to disappoint viewers who—consciously or unconsciously—are aware of all of these obligatory elements and conventions and are expecting them (because part of the fun of watching a genre film is to see how the conventions will play out). The director must decide when to incorporate these elements and conventions as expected and when to twist them in clever or unexpected ways. Likewise, a director must be aware of all of the clichés of a particular genre so he can decide when to embrace them, when to avoid them, and when to subvert or exploit them.

3. The language of film

Over the century of its existence, the cinema has developed its own very specific language. Just as words, grammar, and punctuation have specific meanings and purposes in written language that, when employed properly, allow authors to communicate their ideas to readers, the shots, transitions, and editing in movies also have specific meanings and purposes that let filmmakers communicate their ideas to viewers. Just as a writer needs to know the language he is using to properly tell his stories, a director needs to know the language of film to properly tell his. And so a director needs to be well versed in:

a. The four basic types of shots:

- The Close-up—a shot used to create a sense of intimacy or intensity by emphasizing a character's face or by highlighting a specific action or detail.
- The Medium Shot—a shot used to show characters and action in waist-up views that approximate the usual way we see people and events in real life.
- The Wide Shot—a shot used to show characters and action in full body, to introduce and orient the audience to a setting or location, or to establish the position and relationship of various elements within a scene.

- The Long Shot—a shot used to give an overall view of an immense setting or of large-scale action, to depict landscape, or to convey a sense of massive size and scope.

b. Specialty shots:

- Single—a shot used to highlight or isolate one specific character in a scene.
- Two-shot—a shot used to show two characters relating to one another.
- Over-the-shoulder Shot—a close-up or medium shot of one character filmed over the shoulder (which is visible in the frame) of a second character. An over-the-shoulder shot is used to highlight the featured character while maintaining her/his relationship with the second character and thus create a sense of connectedness and intimacy.
- Low-angle Shot—a shot that frames a character or an object from a low vantage point to create a sense of great size, height, mass, or threat.
- High-angle Shot—a shot that frames a character or an object from a high vantage point to create a sense of diminished size or power.
- Dutch Angle—a tilted shot used to create mystery, tension, uneasiness, or suspense. The Dutch angle gets its name from German ("Deutsche") cinema because it was first used in the German Expressionistic films of the 1910s and the 1920s (films such as *The Cabinet of Dr. Caligari*,

Nosferatu, and *The Last Laugh*). For this reason it is also known as the German angle.

- Crane Shot—a shot made by mounting a camera on a hydraulic lift that can raise the camera from ground level to a point high in the air. It is used to move from a ground-level view of a character or action to a high view or vice versa in a single unedited take.

- Tracking Shot—a shot in which a camera mounted on a moving pedestal (called a dolly) follows a character or an object as it moves through a setting.

- Pan—a shot in which a camera on a fixed pedestal (usually a tripod) is turned from left to right (or vice versa) across a setting to provide a panoramic view of a scene or a setting.

- Tilt—a shot in which a camera on a fixed pedestal is tilted up or down.

- Zoom Shots, Push-ins, and Pull-outs—shots used to move from a wider view to a closer view (or vice versa) in a single shot. Zooms are accomplished by moving a parfocal or varifocal lens to change the view while the camera remains static. Push-ins and pull-outs are accomplished by moving the camera while the lens remains static.

- Insert—a brief close-up of a specific prop (e.g., a newspaper headline) or action (e.g., pocketing a rare coin) that is cut into the main action to make a specific story point.

c. Transitions.

- Transitions refer to the movement from one shot in a movie to the following shot, and from one scene in a movie to the following scene:

- Cut—a straightforward transition from one shot to the next or one scene to the next—one shot or scene ends and the next immediately begins. When a film cuts from one scene to another, it is assumed that the second scene occurs consecutively after the first, with little or no passage of time.

- Dissolve—a transition in which the content of one shot overlaps and is mixed with the content of the following shot for a few seconds until the content of the second shot comes completely to the fore. A dissolve is a more gradual transition than a cut and is usually used to connote the passing of time.

- Wipe—an alternative to a cut or a dissolve in which the content of one shot moves across the face of the previous shot, "wiping" it off the screen.

- Jump Cut—a cut within a shot that removes the middle of the piece and so causes the action of the shot to "jump" from the beginning to the end. A jump cut is a frenetic way to indicate the passage of time.

- Fade In—a shot that begins in black and gradually lightens until the content of the shot is visible. Most movies begin with a fade in.

- Fade Out—a shot in which the image gradually darkens until it becomes black. Most movies end with a fade out.
- Fade Out/Fade In—a transition in the body of a film in which one shot fades to black, which holds for a few seconds and then gradually lightens to reveal the content of the next shot. Fade out/fade ins are usually used to denote the passage of a very long period of time.

d. Montage

Shots are the words of the cinematic language. Transitions are the punctuation. Montage—film editing—is the actual writing. Individual shots can be cut together to create a feeling or an effect (sentences). A series of individual shots can be cut together to form scenes (paragraphs). Scenes can be cut together to form sequences (chapters). And sequences can be cut together to form the entire story. Montage is the process that transforms cinematography into cinema.

4. The core crafts of filmmaking

A director doesn't need to be able to do all the jobs involved in filmmaking, but he does need to be familiar with them and how they can be used to help him tell his story.

- Cinematography—Cinematography is the art and craft of photographing a movie. A director needs to know how shot composition, lighting, and camera movement can be used to convey story points and to create emotion.

- Editing—Editing is the art and craft of assembling individual shots into a complete film. A director must understand how images can be cut together to convey story points and to create emotion.

- Acting—Acting is the craft of portraying a character on-screen. A director does not have to know how to act himself (although many directors begin as actors), but he should be familiar with basic acting techniques so that he can work productively with his cast members to get the best performances possible.

- Production and Costume Design—Production design is the craft of creating and dressing the sets and choosing and dressing the locations where the film will be shot. Costume design is the craft of creating original clothing or selecting preexisting clothing for the actors to wear on-screen. A director needs to be aware of how design can be used to establish setting, tone, and time period and to reflect and enhance characterization.

- Makeup—Makeup is the craft of using cosmetics and other materials to enhance or transform an actor's appearance. A director should have a sense of how makeup can be used to express and reflect character and how it can be enable actors to play various ages, different races and genders, and fantastic or horrifying creatures.

- Special Effects—Special effects are physical gimmicks (bullet hits; explosions; floods; breakaway glass and furniture; flying people on wires; constructing full-scale mechanical sharks and dinosaurs; and so on) deployed on set during filming. A director needs to know how to employ these gimmicks to help tell his tale.

- Stunts—Stuntmen and stuntwomen are specialists who perform actions that are too dangerous or demanding for the actors to attempt themselves without risking injury. A director needs to know how and when to employ a stunt crew to create exciting scenes and sequences without endangering his cast.

- Special Visual Effects—Special visual effects are images used to modify or supplement on-set photography to alter or enhance the appearance of the actors, settings, or cinematography, often to conjure up fantastic worlds, creatures, and action. In years past, special visual effects were created by combining miniatures, models, and matte paintings with various optical processes. In the modern era, they are generated mostly by computer. Computer-generated imagery has become such a ubiquitous and indispensable element in modern filmmaking that no director can do his job properly without having at least some understanding of the techniques of and possibilities offered by CGI.

- Sound—Movie sound is recorded on the set and then augmented in postproduction by additional stock and specially recorded sound effects. A director must know how sound can be recorded, edited, augmented, and mixed to enhance a mood or create an aural setting.

- Music—Film music can be an originally composed and conducted score, existing pieces such as pop songs and classical pieces, or a mixture of both. A director does not have to know how to compose music, but it is helpful if he has a feel for how music can be used to enhance the mood and pacing of a scene, a sequence, and an entire movie.

CHAPTER 4

A Few Skills a Film Director Should Have

There are a number of personal skills that are useful for a film director to have.

1. A director should be organized (or hire someone who can organize him)

There are a lot of things to do and a lot of things to keep track of during the making of a motion picture—meetings, script notes, more meetings, storyboards, even more meetings, auditions, screen tests, location scouts, still more meetings, shoot days, edit days, screenings, meetings, and a lot more meetings. The better organized a director is, the more he will be able to stay on top of his tasks and meet his responsibilities and avoid the feeling that he is—as Francis Ford Coppola once described the hectic quality of making a movie—constantly running down the track in front of a speeding locomotive.

2. A director must be able to prioritize

When juggling all his tasks and duties and responsibilities, a director needs to know which of these things he needs to give his attention to at any given moment and which can wait. For example, sometimes it is more important for a director to consult with the production designer, so that set construction can get under way, than it is for him to cast a supporting part that won't shoot for several more months. Prioritizing is the only way to keep a production running smoothly and efficiently—and the director from being hit by that speeding locomotive.

3. A director must be decisive

The director is a leader of a team. It is the job of team members to suggest ideas to help the director tell the story he wants to tell—the cinematographer suggests ideas about the images, the designers suggest ideas about the sets and costumes, the actors suggest ideas about characterization, and so on—and it is the director's job to accept the ideas that support his vision and veto those that do not. In other words, it is the director's job to decide. Because there are so many people working on a movie and there is so much that has to be accomplished, a director has to make literally hundreds of decisions every day. And he has to make them quickly, or else the entire production will grind to a halt. So a director has to know what he wants and be able to say what he wants without too much dawdling or dithering.

Because the director spends so much of his time dealing/ interacting with others, he must also have strong interpersonal skills.

1. A director must be able to communicate

The director must be able to clearly convey his ideas and wishes to the various members of his team so that they will understand what he wants. A director must also be a good listener so he can hear and clearly comprehend the suggestions his team members make, so that he won't miss out on any excellent ideas that can improve the final product.

2. A director must be able to motivate the members of his team to do their very best

Some insecure helmers attempt to motivate their people through fear—by yelling and screaming, berating them, and throwing tantrums (thus giving rise to the caricature of the raging tyrant director seen in so many Hollywood spoofs), but it's probably safe to assume that people don't do their best work when they are being traumatized. When interviewed, most cinematic craftspeople and technicians confirm they are motivated to do their best work for directors who nurture and inspire them, rather than for those who terrorize them.

3. A director must be able to delegate

Unless it is a micro-budget shoot or a student film, there are simply too many jobs that need to be done in the course of making a movie for one person to do them all. Therefore, a director must hand off vital tasks to others. Because most directors have control-freak tendencies (they wouldn't be directors if they didn't), many of them find this hard to do. While it is not unexpected that directors would want to involve themselves in all aspects of a production, it is best if they can avoid the temptation to micromanage, because doing so can create resentment. (Film crews are made up of working professionals, often with many years of experience in their field. They know what they are doing and object to the impression, created by micromanaging, that they do not. If a director does not trust a member of his team to do a good job, he should replace that person with someone he does trust and let them get on with it.) Like indecision, micromanaging can cause the production process to grind to a halt. On most projects, effective delegation by the director makes for a smoother production, a happier crew, and a better final product.

4. A director must be politically adept

Moviemaking can be a very political endeavor. There are often many different factions at work on a film—from the studio level to the production offices to the floor of the set—each of which wants something for itself (money, control, creative satisfaction, credit and acclaim, etc.) out of the process. These blocs and their agendas can interfere with the director's ability to make the movie he wants to make in the way he wants to make it, so it behooves the helmer to be able to recognize the various cliques at work inside and outside the production and to know how to charm, coax, cajole, persuade, unite, and sometimes even bully them into letting him do what he wants and needs to do.

CHAPTER 5

Getting the Job

Before a director can direct a movie, he must first have a movie to direct. There are several ways for a helmer to land a project:

DIY

Independent directors will often create their own projects. They will write their own scripts (or get people to write scripts for them), and then look for funding for the production (from independent film companies, from professional backers both inside and outside the film business, by soliciting funds on crowd-funding websites such as Kickstarter, or by appealing to sympathetic relatives and friends) or finance it themselves (by using their own income, by maxing out credit cards, and sometimes by selling their own blood), shoot the film, complete it, and then go looking for a distributor—often by entering the finished product in festivals and competitions such as Sundance.

Development

Established directors with their own production companies will frequently develop projects that interest them. A director who does this will either come up with an idea himself or find a script or other piece of material (such as a book or a magazine article) that he likes, sell it to a studio, and then work to assemble all the necessary elements (a finely honed screenplay, a bankable cast, a talented creative team, and a capable production crew) in the hope that the studio will green-light (approve for production) the project and make the movie.

Taking an assignment

Established directors are often offered projects by producers, production companies, and studios. In other instances, directors will go after jobs that interest them—usually high-profile studio movies. For these gigs, a director will meet with the producer or studio executives to express his enthusiasm for the proposed movie and his desire to direct it, and to then present his ideas for bringing the project to the screen. Many of these meetings are simple conversations, but sometimes a director will go further and craft elaborate presentations—often consisting of written documents, specially prepared artwork, or even lavishly produced short films—to demonstrate how he would realize the film in the hope that the producer or the studio will select him for the assignment.

The DGA

Directors who make movies for the major film studios and production companies must be or become members of the Directors Guild of America. The DGA is a craft union that represents directors (and members of the directorial team) in all media in the United States. The Directors Guild negotiates agreements with studios, production companies, and producers covering pay and working conditions for its members. Those agreements stipulate that only guild members may direct projects for signatory companies. The DGA also runs training programs to help newcomers break into the industry, and gives awards to its members for outstanding work. Many other countries have their own unions for directors.

CHAPTER 6

The Film Director in Preproduction

Once a director has a project to work on, preproduction—the process of preparing the movie for filming—begins.

A helmer has a lot to do during preproduction. What follows is an overview of the tasks a director needs to attend to before shooting begins:

Conceive a vision

Before any other serious preparatory work can be done, a director must develop a vision for the production—a concept for realizing the film on screen. This concept is vital because it will influence every aspect of the film, from the shooting script to the production design to casting to cinematography to editing, sound, and music.

The director's vision should include the following elements:

1. *A theme:* a core notion of what the film is about—a guiding idea of what the story is meant to say and what dramatic point it is intended to make.

2. *A storytelling style:* Will the tale be told in a realistic manner or will it be stylized in some fashion (e.g., will the tone be melodramatic or campy or larger than life)? Will the action be believably down to earth or outrageously over the top? Will the comedy be subtle or broad? Will the sex or violence be discreet or graphic? Will the pace of the storytelling be lyrically slow or pulse-poundingly fast?

3. *A visual concept:* Will the movie be photographed in black and white or color? If it is shot in color, will the palate be desaturated, lifelike, or heightened? Will the lighting be natural or dramatic—overly flat or full of shadows and contrast? Will the shot compositions be loose or formal? Will the camera move or will it be static? Will the editing allow shots to unfold in long, leisurely fashion or will they be presented in quick, rapid-fire cuts?

Form a working relationship with the producer

The director and the producer work together to get the movie made. On paper, the director is responsible for the creative aspects of the production and the producer is responsible for everything else—finances, logistics, politics (especially when dealing with the studio), and promotion—but in reality things are never that cut-and-dried. The producer usually has a say (sometimes quite a significant one, especially if he initiated the project) in creative matters and—because making art is always subject to practicalities, the director cannot help but become involved in the producer's purview.

Ideally, the two will respect and support one another in attending to their duties and responsibilities. If they do, then their partnership can become a stimulating and productive collaboration. If not, then the professional marriage between director and producer can lead to tension and sometimes a struggle for creative control of the film (to avoid this, many successful directors eventually opt to become their own producers).

Collaborate on a schedule and budget

As previously mentioned, the producer is generally responsible for the financial and logistical aspects of the moviemaking process. The producer himself usually takes care of the broader elements of the production—acquiring the core material; assembling the talent package (the director, the screenwriter, and the stars); raising the money to make the movie; and securing a distribution deal—and then hires a team to assist him with the nuts and bolts of the production.

The key members of the production team are:

- Line Producer—The line producer is initially responsible for drawing up a budget and devising a schedule for the project. He then oversees all the physical and practical aspects of the production—securing soundstages and shooting locations; hiring below-the-line (noncreative) crew members; renting or buying necessary equipment, material, and supplies; transporting, housing, and feeding the cast and crew; troubleshooting problems; and generally making certain that everyone and everything required to make the movie is where it needs to be when it needs to be with a minimum of fuss and bother. Above all, the line producer is responsible for working with the director, the producer, and the crew to make sure filming stays on schedule and on budget. Line producers are sometimes credited as Executive Producers.

- Unit Production Manager—The unit production manager has essentially the same duties and responsibilities as the line producer (in fact, on many productions, one person functions as both the line producer and the UPM.). The differences are mostly of degree and emphasis—the line producer is usually concerned with the overall production, while the unit production manager is focused more on day-to-day operations. Large-scale films usually employ both a line producer and a production manager, while smaller projects often only employ a UPM.

- First Assistant Director—The first assistant director's primary responsibilities come during production—he prepares the daily call sheets (an official schedule and list of all of the personnel, equipment, and props required for the particular day's work); makes sure all cast, crew, and equipment are on hand and in position when needed; moves the crew from setup to setup in an efficient, orderly manner that keeps the production on schedule; tends to the feeding, health, and safety of the cast and crew; and prepares daily reports on the progress of the filming for the producer and studio. Although the first AD does most of his work during filming, he is usually brought onto a project during preproduction because his years of on-set experience make him very good at estimating how long it takes to shoot various types of scenes, expertise that can prove invaluable in devising a realistic shooting schedule for the picture.

During preproduction, the director collaborates with the production team to hash out a reasonable budget—one that can provide the director with enough resources to satisfactorily realize his vision, but at a price the financiers can live with. Depending on the project, professional film budgets can run anywhere from ten thousand to several hundred million dollars.

The director and the production team also collaborate on a workable schedule for the movie—one that gives the director enough days to comfortably shoot all the required scenes while keeping the production within budget. Since shooting days are expensive (running anywhere from $5,000 a day to several million, depending on the type of film) the number can frequently become a matter of contention—directors (who want as much time as possible to get things right) usually want more, and producers (who understandably need to watch every penny) always want less. Film schedules can be as short as three weeks or as long as six to eight months.

A director pushes for a schedule that accommodates his creative needs. For example, he may want to shoot an intense emotional scene between the two leads at the end of the shoot to give the actors a few weeks to get to know one another and develop an off-screen relationship that will hopefully enhance the on-screen one. Or he may want to shoot the film in sequence to allow the drama and performances to develop naturally. On the flip side, the production team wants the schedule to be as practical and economical as possible—e.g., to shoot all the scenes that take place in a particular setting at the same time, to save the days and money it would cost to come back again and again.

There is a lot of give and take in this process and a great deal of compromising on both sides. A director must be sure he can live with the results—that he has enough time and resources to properly make the movie the way he sees fit—and not just to ensure that he can achieve creative satisfaction. In most instances, directors are required as part of their contracts to abide by the final agreed-upon budget and schedule. If they don't—if they go sufficiently over schedule or run considerably over budget—they can face legal and financial penalties (including being responsible for cost overages).

Revise the script

During preproduction, the director also works with the screenwriter to get the screenplay ready for filming.

If the movie is based on an original idea by the director or one of his associates, or if it is based on a piece of material (a novel, a play, a magazine article, etc.) the director has acquired to adapt into a movie, then he will work with the writer from inception to ensure the final shooting script represents his concept for the project (and, of course, if he's penning the script himself, then he's doing this automatically). If the movie is based on an existing screenplay (one the director has acquired for himself or that he has been hired to make), then he will work with the screenwriter to rewrite that script—sometimes lightly and sometimes quite extensively—into one that reflects his vision for the project.

Directors work with screenwriters in different ways. Some stick with the same writer from the beginning of the writing process to the end; others employ multiple scribes throughout the writing and rewriting. A director will usually replace a screenwriter if he feels that he and the writer aren't in sync creatively or if he feels that the writer isn't

able (or willing—screenwriters can be as stubborn as directors) to give him what he wants. Some directors may bring
in a string of writers to pound away at the script until they
get the results they are after. Others like to employ different writers to handle various elements of the script—one to
work on plot, another to craft the action, an additional scribe
to enhance characterization, and yet another to polish the
dialogue. Some directors don't bring in any additional writers at all, but instead make the desired changes themselves.

Many screenwriters dislike the fact that some directors
will use so many scribes on a single project—they feel that
it is disrespectful to their craft and minimizes their role in
the filmmaking process by making them seem disposable.
However, in the modern film industry, the director has the
last creative word—so if the helmer and the scripter don't
see eye to eye, it is the screenwriter who must give way.

Analyze the script

Once the screenplay is complete (or almost complete), most
directors will do a comprehensive dramatic analysis of the
piece.

A director will usually begin with an overview of the complete narrative to get a sense of the overall dramatic shape of
the piece by identifying the spine of the story (i.e., determining where the key structural moments—introduction of the
protagonist, inciting incident, Act I plot twist, establishment

of the protagonist's goal, initiation of the conflict with the antagonist, Act II plot twist, climax, and resolution—are located); by getting a feel for the overall rhythm, flow, and pace of the piece; and by determining what its theme or themes are.

The director will then do an in-depth analysis of each individual scene in the script to get a firm handle on how it fits in to the overall story: what its purpose is in the plot; how it helps propel the narrative; and how it relates to the theme. This analysis will help the director when it comes time to shoot the scene, because it will tell him what the focus of the segment should be; what aspects of the scene to emphasize and which to play down; what the dramatic mood and tone should be; and how the scene should be paced.

Assemble the creative team

During preproduction the director assembles his creative team—the talented and experienced people who will help him realize all the various elements of the film. The creative team includes the:

- Cinematographer—also known as the Director of Photography (or the DP or the cameraman). The cinematographer is in charge of photographing the movie. The director works with the cinematographer to determine the photographic style of the film—an approach to the lighting, shot composition, camera movement, image quality, and color palette that will best express the director's concept. They also decide which aspect ratio (the width and height of the image when it is projected on screen—1.85:1 and 2.39:1 are the most common) to use and if the movie will be shot with one camera or several. (Multiple cameras are often used when the material being photographed cannot easily be restaged or repeated—big crowd scenes, complicated action and effects sequences, an unusually intense performance scene, and so on.)

- Editor—the editor assembles all the individual shots made during production into a cohesive whole. The editor is arguably the director's most vital creative collaborator, since he helps determine the final shape of the movie.

- Production Designer—the production designer creates the settings in which the film will be shot. The director and the production designer work together to determine which scenes will be filmed on constructed sets and which will be filmed in real locations. The production designer then designs the sets and supervises their construction and dressing. He also helps select the real-world locations and dresses them appropriately. All the production designer's work is focused on reflecting the directorial concept.

- Costume Designer—the costume designer creates or acquires all the clothing the actors will wear in the movie. As with the cinematographer and the production designer, all the costume designer's creative choices are made in accordance with the director's vision.

- Creative Makeup Designer—if the story calls for an actor's appearance to be significantly altered—when the performer must be aged, maimed, made to resemble a famous historical figure, or transformed into a fantastical creature—then the director will call in a creative makeup designer to devise and implement the alteration. A creative makeup designer uses prosthetics, silicone, foam rubber, and other devices and materials to remake an actor's appearance.

- Composer—the composer creates original music for the film (and usually orchestrates and conducts it, as well). The composer usually doesn't start working until the postproduction period, but is brought on early if any original music is required to be played on set during filming.

- Sound Designer—the sound designer is responsible for creating all the sound effects heard in the film apart from the music and dialogue. He edits together the sounds recorded on the set during production and new sounds created in postproduction to create an aural environment that supports and complements the film's imagery.

- Special Effects Supervisor—the special effects supervisor oversees the creation and implementation of the on-set special effects. During preproduction, the director and FX supervisor will meet to determine what effects the film will require, how long it will take to prepare and shoot them, and what safety precautions and other on-set accommodations will be required to carry them out. The director will use this information to adjust his shooting plan accordingly.

- Stunt Coordinator—the stunt coordinator, who is usually a stuntperson himself, assembles the stunt team, devises and prepares the specific stunts, and then oversees their execution during filming. The stunt coordinator also choreographs fight scenes, car chases, and other elaborate action involving people. As with the special effects supervisor, the director will usually meet with the stunt coordinator well in advance of shooting to determine what stunts the movie requires, how long they will take to prepare and shoot, and what precautions and accommodations will be required to bring them off safely during filming.

- Visual Effects Supervisor—the director will work with the VFX supervisor to determine which scenes will require visual effects. The two will collaborate on the design of the effects and work out what live-action material the director needs to film as component pieces for the FX shots (e.g., filming actors in front of a green screen so that they can later be composited into a VFX shot) and determine what special effects need to be employed during the live-action shooting (e.g., the use of a wind machine to simulate a giant creature's breath; the use of interactive lighting to simulate the effect of a laser blast; and so on) to "sell" the VFX that will be added later.

- Second Unit Director—when a film contains a great deal of stunt work or action sequences (car chases, battle scenes, and so on)—complex, highly technical sequences that take a long time to plan and shoot—the production will often set up a second production unit—complete with its own camera crew and production team—to film this material concurrently with the main unit, so that the movie can be finished in a reasonable amount of time. Second units are also used to shoot background footage for films set in exotic locales or inserts or fill-in material for scenes shot by the main unit. The second unit has its own director, who can sometimes be the main unit's editor, cinematographer, or stunt coordinator, but many times an outside director is brought in. The director selects the second unit director and then designs and prepares the second unit sequences with him. Most second unit scenes are filmed without the main cast and use stunt doubles instead. However, if any shots of the principals are required for a second unit sequence—close-ups of the leading man at the wheel during a car chase, for example—that material is filmed by the director.

Once the director has selected these key members of his creative team, he puts them to work. The team members (often called department heads) will assemble their own individual crews and then generate ideas based on the director's vision for the director to approve. Sometimes extensive test shooting will be done to determine how well these approved ideas work on film, and ideas may be altered or thrown out entirely based on the results. Once all ideas and concepts have been approved, preparations are made to implement or realize them during production.

Cast the actors

One of the most important things a director does during preproduction is cast the movie—select actors to play roles in the story. Casting is very important because most directors agree that the key factor in obtaining a great performance is to select the right actor to play the part. A professional casting director is usually hired to help the director with this vital task. A casting director is familiar with the available talent pool and is always on the lookout for new and emerging actors, and so is in a position to offer the director informed and viable suggestions for filling the film's many large and small roles. The casting director also has strong relationships with actors' representatives (agents and managers) and so can easily facilitate meetings and auditions.

Sometimes the director will want a star to play a certain part. Most big-name actors do not audition, so the director will send the screenplay to the star and—if the star likes the script—meet with him or her to discuss the role. If the discussion goes well, negotiations between the star's representatives and the production will commence and will hopefully lead to the star taking the part. If not, the search will continue until the role is cast.

Well-known character actors are often approached to play important supporting parts in the same way. Lesser-known and unknown actors are usually required to audition for parts so that directors can get a sense of their range and abilities and so they can see how well (or not) the actors can take direction. Directors will sometimes shoot screen tests of promising candidates to see how they look on film, to further assess their acting abilities, or to see if they have sufficient chemistry with other actors in the film (this is especially important for love stories).

Once the primary cast is assembled, the director will usually gather the actors to read through the script aloud, so that everyone can get a feel for the piece and the chemistry of the ensemble. Most film budgets do not allow for any sort of extensive rehearsal in advance of shooting (since paying actors the extra money required for rehearsals can increase the cost of the film considerably), although some successful directors with clout can and do insist upon them. If no rehearsals are possible, then the director will still spend time with the actors discussing their roles in depth, so that everyone will have a clear idea of what they want the characters to be.

Scout locations

If any part of the movie is going to be shot outside the studio, the director, the cinematographer, and production designer will travel about looking for real-world locations that suit the story and the director's conception. They will do this in conjunction with the production team to ensure the locations will be both artistically correct and practical— that they will be reasonably accessible to personnel and equipment; that they are relatively close to proper food and lodging for the crew; that they are cost-effective; and so on.

Storyboard and previz

Many directors like to prepare for a shoot by storyboarding—i.e., drawing each shot they envision for a scene on paper like a comic strip. Storyboarding helps the director develop the visual feel and flow of the scene and helps him clearly communicate his ideas to the crew. Some directors will storyboard every scene in the movie. Others will only storyboard big action scenes or special effects sequences— segments of the film that contain a lot of complex technical elements and require a great deal of preplanning to properly execute. This allows everyone involved in making these scenes to know exactly what results are expected and what they need to do to prepare accordingly.

In recent years, storyboards have been sometimes supplemented and frequently supplanted by a process known as "previsualization" or "previz" for short. Previz consists of rudimentary computer-generated shots that provide a much fuller depiction of the action and movement the director wants in a shot than it is possible for the static images in storyboards to convey. Previz has become a foundational element in the planning of most visual effects sequences and an increasingly common one in the planning of stunt and action scenes.

Preshoot

Movies will often use filmed material as part of a scene—TV news reports, commercials, film clips, graphics, and so on. All this material is shot during preproduction so it will be ready to be used on set during production.

Because so many key decisions affecting the film's style and content are made during preproduction, this period is arguably the most important period in the making of a movie.

Once preproduction is completed, it is time for the director to begin shooting.

CHAPTER 7

The Film Director in Principal Photography

Principal photography is the phase of the filmmaking process during which the movie is shot. It is the most intense and expensive part of moviemaking, and the director is at the white-hot center of it all.

Preparing the day's work

The director prepares for each day of principal photography by determining the business (the actions and behavior) the actors will perform in the scene or scenes scheduled to be filmed, and by working out the blocking (where the actors will be positioned in the set and how they will move about during the scene).

One of the most important parts of a director's preparation is to plan his coverage—to devise the shots he will need to properly record (or "cover") the scene or scenes. The standard approach to covering a scene is to first film a master shot—a wide shot in which the entire set is visible and in which the actors perform the scene from beginning to end. The master provides a base for the scene. The director then moves in tighter for medium shots, over-the-shoulder shots, close-ups, and inserts—shots that will emphasize and detail various parts of the action. Not every director films a scene in exactly this way—some cover the entire scene in a single shot; others eschew master shots; and so on. But however a director approaches it, the goal is to collect enough material to assemble a scene that is both narratively and visually coherent and interesting.

Some directors do their preparation days, weeks, or even months in advance of shooting—often via the storyboarding or previz process. As mentioned in the previous chapter, advance preparation is mandatory for big action and special effects sequences. However, there are directors who like to extensively preplan the movie's "smaller" scenes—those focused primarily on the actors' performances—as well. (The legendary Alfred Hitchcock was famous for working out every detail of every shot of every scene of his pictures long before filming began. His preparation was so complete that he often said he felt as if he had already made the movie and that the actual filming was something of an afterthought.)

When this type of director arrives on the set, he instructs the crew where to place the camera, tells the actors where to stand and what to do, and then gets on with it—requiring everyone to accommodate themselves to his preconceived business, blocking, and camera angles. The advantage to this approach is that it can get the workday off to a fast start and enable it to proceed with extreme efficiency. The disadvantage is that the results can sometimes feel a bit stiff and lacking in spontaneity.

Other directors prefer to wait until the day a performance-based scene is being filmed to prepare it. A helmer who takes this approach will begin by having the actors run through the scene on the set. The director will give the performers a free hand so he can see where their instincts will take them—allowing them to discover and invent their own bits of business and find their own rudimentary blocking. The director will then work with the actors to refine and shape what they have done into a fully realized scene. Only after this is done will he devise his coverage—accommodating the shots to the scene, rather than the scene to the shots. (Sidney Lumet, the famed director of *Serpico* and *Dog Day Afternoon*, favored this method.) The disadvantage to this approach is that it can take longer for the workday to get started, but the advantage is that the scenes often feel much more natural and alive.

No matter how he goes about preparing a scene, a director must always address a number of important issues:

- He must be sure he is clearly and effectively presenting all the scene's intended story and character points.
- He must be sure he is laying out the geography of the scene—devising shots that show the audience where all

the important elements of the set (doors, windows, furniture, and so on) are located and where the characters are positioned when the scene begins—so that viewers will have a clear sense of the physical space the action is taking place in and be able to comprehend where characters are coming from and where they are going.

• He must be sure he is milking the scene for all it is worth—wringing out of it all of the comedy, drama, romance, or thrills he possibly can.

A director's preparation must be thorough and complete, but it must never become a straitjacket. Every day that a movie is in production, the director is at the head of a vast army of artists, craftspeople, and technicians with a very expensive clock ticking constantly. Obviously, he must have a very clearly defined plan for where he wants to lead them and how he wants them to get there. On the other hand, he must also remain flexible—open and available to the in-the-moment inspiration and happy accidents that can make a movie truly come alive.

The shot list

However a director prepares, he will eventually come up with a list of shots that the unit will need to film to complete the day's scheduled work. The director will then confer with the cinematographer, the unit production manager, and the first assistant director to determine the best order in which to film those shots. This order is usually set with an eye on efficiency and practicality. For example, all shots that face the same way may be filmed together no matter what order they appear in the scene, so they can all use the same lighting setup (since lighting must be adjusted—which can be a time-consuming process—whenever the camera is moved more than fifteen degrees). Or close-ups of the actors may be filmed first thing in the morning, so the performers will look fresh when they are photographed (rather than tired, as they might after a long day's work), and so on.

Setting up the first shot

Once the shot order has been determined, the crew will set up the first shot of the day—the cinematographer will work with his team to light the set and position the camera, while the set dressers and the prop, special effects, and costume and makeup crews will attend to their duties. If there are any extras (actors who appear in the background of shots but do not have any lines), the first assistant director will give them their business and blocking.

Working with the actors

While the first shot is being set up, the director will usually spend some time rehearsing the scene with the cast.

Working with actors is one of the most important parts of a film director's job. It's a task that requires great flexibility—every actor has his or her own unique approach to the craft, so for a director to get the best out of his cast, he needs to work with each actor according to his or her own technique rather than applying a one-size-fits-all method.

A director must also be a bit of a psychologist. Actors are notoriously sensitive creatures (they have to be—their job requires them to keep their feelings close to the surface and ready to be summoned at a moment's notice). A good director will learn how to tend to his performers' emotional states so that they can make their feelings work for them, rather than get in the way.

Some directors take a dictatorial approach with thespians—telling them exactly what to do and how to do it, even to the point of giving them line readings (instructing them how to perform each and every word of dialogue). Most actors do not respond well to this tactic—they feel it straitjackets them, marginalizes their talents and contributions, and makes it difficult for them to give a fully living and breathing performance. Actors usually prefer directors to give them the freedom to act out the scene the way they think is best and then work with them to adjust and temper that performance until they arrive at a satisfying result.

Some actors like to improvise. It is up to the director to decide if this is appropriate for a scene or a film or if the actors should stick to the script.

Actors want a director to protect them—to create a safe environment for them to experiment with different (and sometimes quite extreme) approaches to a scene or performance on the way to a final product without being made to feel foolish. Actors also want a director to protect them by not allowing anything into the final cut of a film that will embarrass them. If the performers feel they can trust their director to look out for them, then they will be more willing and able to give their all, which can only make the movie better.

Filming the first shot

After the crew has finished setting up the first shot, the director will review the various components of the piece and make any changes or adjustments he feels are required. Sometimes he will have the actors and the camera and effects crews rehearse the action a few times to get the feel and the timing just right.

Once the director is satisfied that everything is correct, filming begins. The first assistant director calls for quiet on the set; the actors take their starting positions; the camera and sound recorder are turned on; and when they are both rolling at the proper speed, the director calls for "Action!" and the actors begin performing the scene.

The director watches the scene unfold, focusing intently on the performances and everything else playing out in front of the camera. In earlier times, the director would watch from a position very near the camera, so that he could get an approximate sense of how the scene would appear in the shot. These days, however, most movie cameras have a video assist—a tap that transmits the exact image the camera is photographing to a television monitor. The monitor is usually set up in an encampment away from the camera called the "video village," so most directors will watch from there instead.

When the scene is over, the director will call "Cut!" and filming will stop. (Only the director can call cut—it is a grave offense for anyone else on the set to do so, unless the director has given them permission.)

Each filmed version of a shot is called a "take." If the director is satisfied with the first take, then the work on the first shot is finished. If the director is not satisfied, he will call for another take and continue to do so—making adjustments in performances and other elements—until he gets the results he wants.

The number of takes is often an issue of contention— directors often want to be able to do as many as necessary to get a shot right. However, since every minute spent in production is enormously expensive, the production team will always prefer that the director do as few takes as possible.

Once work on the first shot is completed, the director will select the takes he likes and order them to be printed so that they can be reviewed and then turned over to the editor. (This is only if the movie is being shot on film. If it is being shot digitally, no printing is required. However, the director will still indicate which takes he prefers.)

The unit then moves on and begins setting up the next shot on the list. The first assistant director supervises this process. Aided by a team of second and third assistant directors and production assistants, he moves the company along as efficiently and briskly as possible.

Between setups

It can take anywhere from a few minutes to a several hours to set up a shot, depending on how complex it is. The director uses this time to attend to other things:

- He will continue to work with the actors.
- He will prep for shots to be done later that day.
- He will review and approve plans, concepts, and work being done by the creative and production teams in preparation for scenes that will be shot later in the schedule.
- He may continue to work on the screenplay. Moviemaking is a fluid process—things are always changing, and

the director may want the script altered to incorporate new ideas; to add, revise, or delete lines of dialogue, bits of business, and entire scenes and sequences; to beef up roles (if an actor proves to be especially terrific and the director wants to give him more to do) or pare them down (if an actor proves to be especially not terrific and the director wants to give him less to do); or to accommodate unexpected things that happen during filming. (The ending of *Jaws* was famously reworked because director Steven Spielberg wanted to include a spectacular but unplanned shot of a shark destroying a diving cage that was filmed by the second unit. In the original script, Richard Dreyfuss's character was supposed to be in the cage when the shark attacked and would get killed, but in the actual shot, the cage was empty. So the script was rewritten and, as a result, Dreyfuss survived.)

Some directors keep the original (or final) screenwriter on the set with them to make these changes. Others don't want the writer on the set (because they don't want the writer questioning what they are doing). These directors will work with the writer over the phone or by email. Or they may bring in a completely different writer. Or make the required changes themselves. Or wing it by improvising solutions with the cast or crew.

- At some point during the workday, the director will screen dailies—footage shot on the previous day by the main unit, as well as material shot by the second and other units. This is done to check the quality of the work, to select the takes the director wants to use in the final movie, and to determine if there's anything that needs to be reshot or any additional material that needs to be filmed.

Tone

The director sets the tone on the set—some prefer a crisp, efficient, no-nonsense work environment, while others encourage a more loose and informal atmosphere. Some helmers take a dictatorial approach to their work—barking out commands and rebuffing all outside input—while others are more inclusive and collaborative. Some directors yell and scream; others are quiet and soft-spoken. Is one of these approaches better than the others? It's hard to say—certainly cast and crews prefer helmers who are more easy-going, but great films have been made by directors working in all of these styles.

Continuity

As filming continues on all the shots that will ultimately be joined together to create a single scene, the director must pay close attention to the continuity—the matching of components—between shots.

For a scene to cut together smoothly, all of the components—lighting, action, dialogue, costumes, prop placement, and so on—in all of the shots must be consistent. If they are not (e.g., if the light is coming from above in one shot and from the side in the next; if an actor is wearing a blue tie in one shot and a brown tie in another; if a shot of the actor holding a gun in his right hand is followed by one of him holding it in his left; etc.), then the discrepancies will be immediately apparent when the shots are put together, and the illusion that they are all pieces of the same whole will be lost. The audience will be distracted by this and pulled instantly out of the story.

One very important element of continuity is the "180-degree rule"—the notion that there is an imaginary line that divides the set and connects the characters in a scene. When filming all the shots in a scene, the camera must be consistently positioned on the same side of the line. This ensures that when the shots are intercut, a character on the right side of the frame in the first shot will remain on the right side of the frame throughout the entire scene and a character on the left side of the frame will remain on the left. This will create a consistent on-screen spatial relationship between the characters and between the characters and the setting. If the camera is placed on the opposite side of the line (a gaffe known as "crossing the line" or "jumping the line") for any shot in the sequence, when the shots are cut together the characters will bounce from one side of the frame to the next. Their spatial relationships with the other characters and with the setting will be destroyed and, once again, the illusion that all of the shots are pieces of the same whole will be lost. This inconsistency can confuse and disorient the audience.

The 180-degree rule also applies to movement within the frame. Characters, vehicles, and objects must always move in the same direction (from the left side of the frame to the right, and so on) in every shot in a sequence so that when they are all put together, the characters, vehicles, and objects will always appear to be heading the same way on-screen. If the 180-degree rule is not observed, then the characters, vehicles, or objects will switch directions with every cut and the scene's visual coherence will be destroyed.

Eyelines are another key element of continuity—actors must look in the exact same direction in every shot, so that when the scene is put together, the actors will always appear to be looking toward the same place or at the same thing for the duration of the sequence.

Some directors will deliberately shatter continuity for creative reasons (e.g., to create a sense of dislocation and disorientation), but in most cases, it is the director's goal to create visually coherent scenes and sequences, and so he must make continuity a factor when creating and executing shots. He is assisted in this task by a crew member called the script supervisor, whose primary responsibility is to maintain a scene's continuity from shot to shot and the film's continuity from scene to scene.

The script supervisor does this by taking detailed notes (often supplemented with photographs) concerning every element in every shot in a scene or sequence, including: the length of the shot; the action that occurs in the shot; the positioning of the actors and of key props and set dressing (such as the furniture); the clothes and hairstyles the actors are wearing, as well as their condition (neat, messy, etc.); the screen direction of any movement of people, vehicles, and objects; the exact dialogue each actor speaks in each take (including flubs); the way the shot is lit and the lens used to film it; and so on. The script supervisor shares these notes with all the key teams (camera, lighting, sound, costumes, makeup, props, and special effects) working on set so they can make sure all of the elements remain consistent from shot to shot as the scene is filmed. If the script supervisor is capable, then the director can be assured that continuity will be maintained and so can direct the bulk of his attention elsewhere.

The script supervisor assists the director in several other ways, including:

- Recording information about each take of each shot in the screenplay—marking down the number of the take (which is also written on the sound and picture slates that appear at the head of every take); indicating which portion of the script each shot covers; writing down the director's comments on each take—which are good, which are bad, which should be printed, which he wants the editor to use, and so on. The director and editor use all this information later when they are cutting the picture.

- Keeping the script current by incorporating all rewrites; marking down any changes to the dialogue or action made during filming; and so on.
- Preparing daily progress reports for the director, production team, and studio that include a record of the pages, scenes, and minutes that were shot that day, the amount of script that has been filmed to date, and the amount that remains to be completed.

Making the day

Creatively, the director's job during production is to get the results he wants and needs from each scene to make the movie he has envisioned. Practically, his job is to "make the day"—to film every scene or portion of a scene scheduled for each day of production on that day without going into overtime (and thus exceeding the budget).

Every movie budget anticipates some overtime and the possibility of exceeding the schedule by a few days, but if production begins to fall significantly behind schedule or go significantly over budget—either for reasons within the director's control (the speed at which he is working, the

lengths he will go to achieve perfection) or beyond it (problems with the weather, a cast member falling ill, equipment
trouble)—then it is the director's responsibility to work with
the production team to find ways to catch up and get back on
schedule. Doing so can involve limiting the number of takes,
cutting out shots, dropping effects, or even eliminating entire scenes or sequences. The challenge is to implement such
measures without hurting the quality of the finished film.

Sometimes this isn't possible, and then the director, producer, and studio may opt to deliberately go over budget.
This is always a risky proposition—if the final film is a big
financial success, then most times, all is forgiven. However,
if an over-budget film only breaks even or is a failure, the
director's career may be impeded or entirely derailed, so
this is a step that should be taken only when there is no
other option.

Wrapping up

When the last take of the last shot is finished, the day's work
is over. This process repeats itself every day until principal
photography is complete.

CHAPTER 8

The Film Director in Postproduction

After principal photography has been completed, the film moves into postproduction—the completion phase of moviemaking.

Directors may continue to shoot during postproduction—they may need to film pickups (extra shots needed to complete a scene that could not be filmed during principal photography) or inserts; live-action elements for visual effects shots; additional action sequences; and so on. They may also continue to supervise the production of visual effects (because VFX take so long to generate, work on them usually continues well into post).

However, the director's primary focus during postproduction is on . . .

Editing

During principal photography, the director will select the takes he prefers of each shot and turn them over to the editor, who will string them together into an assembly—a collection of all of the shots filmed for the movie in approximate narrative order. The editor will then start cutting the individual shots together to create proper scenes and sequences and, not long after principal photography is finished, will have readied a rough cut—a rudimentary (and usually much too long) version of the movie that follows the script as closely as possible.

Free from the pressures of production and now able to give his full attention to the finishing process, the director then joins the editor and together they begin refining the rough cut into a new version called the director's cut. (All directors working under a DGA contract have the right to create one version of the film that is exactly the way they want it to be. This is called the director's cut.)

As the director works on his cut, he needs to be as objective as possible about the footage at hand. Moviemaking is a fluid, unpredictable process, and no matter how well planned or carefully executed, things do not always turn out as originally intended—sometimes they turn out much better (an actor in a minor role gives a performance that unexpectedly lights up the screen); sometimes they turn out much worse (a comic set piece or action sequence falls disappointingly flat); sometimes they just turn out differently (a dramatic scene generates some surprising but effective laughs; a comedic scene provokes some unforeseen but quite moving emotion). So, the greatest challenge a director faces during editing is to embrace the movie he shot, rather than the one he had hoped to shoot—to see the footage for what it is rather than for what he hoped it would be. By doing so, he can then concentrate on making the film the best it can be, rather than on forcing it to be something it is not.

As the director and the editor put the movie together, they may find that some of the scenes cut together exactly as originally conceived; that others may need to be completely rethought and reworked; that many need to be shortened; and that a few need to be dropped entirely (because they are redundant; because they slow down the movie's pace; or because they simply don't work). When considering the overall narrative, the director and editor may discover that it plays exactly as scripted or they may discover that the order of scenes and events need to be partially or entirely rearranged for the story to work effectively. They may decide to focus more on some characters and less on others. They may opt to cut back on exposition and to emphasize the comedy, the horror, the romance, or the thrills. Eventually, after much creative exertion and invention, the director's cut—the helmer's definitive vision of the movie he made—finally emerges.

At this point, the director will screen the movie for the producer and studio executives, who will then offer their suggestions for changes, fixes, and improvements. What happens next depends on the director's contract.

Some very successful or very independent helmers have the right to final cut written into their agreements. Final cut means that no changes can be made to the director's cut without his approval. So, if the director has final cut, then he will accept whatever suggestions he finds valid, reject the others, and that will be the end of it. If the director does not have final cut, then the people who own the movie—the producer or the studio (or the backers, if it's an independent film)—have the legal right to do with it what they please.

When the director doesn't have final cut and the producer or studio wants changes made that he doesn't want to make, he has several options: he can make the changes under protest; he can try to talk the producer and studio out of making the changes; he can refuse to make the changes and hope the producer and the studio back down; he can refuse to make the changes and get fired; he can quit. If the director gets fired or quits, the producer will usually make the alterations. If the director is sufficiently unhappy with the results, he can petition the DGA to have his name taken off the finished film (if his petition is approved, then his name will be replaced in the credits by a pseudonym—for years, "Alan Smithee" was the most commonly used alias for disgruntled directors).

The director quitting or getting fired are worst-case scenarios. Usually both sides compromise and come up with alternative changes that everyone can live with, even if they're not thrilled with them.

Previews

At some point—usually when the director's cut or the producer/studio version is complete—the movie will be test-screened for members of the general public so that the filmmakers can see how it plays. (If there is strong disagreement between the director and the producer or studio over the director's cut, both the helmer's version and the producer/studio iteration may be screened to see which one the audiences prefer.)

The filmmakers will carefully observe the reactions of the viewers during the test screening. Are they laughing in the right places? Are they scared when they should be? Are they crying at the end? After the screening, the audience members will be asked to fill out survey cards indicating how much they liked or disliked certain characters and specific elements of the movie. The results will be analyzed, and changes may be made to the movie to correct elements that receive a strong negative response.

Reshoots

Sometimes those corrections are made by reediting the movie—by recutting scenes, rearranging them, or removing them. Sometimes the decision is made to reshoot certain scenes or to film new material (including, most frequently, a new ending, if the test audience is sufficiently unhappy with the existing one) in order to clarify, enhance, or otherwise improve the picture. In that case, the director will supervise the development, preparation, and shooting of the new material in the same way that he did for the original production (unless he has quit or been fired, at which point a new director will be brought in to do the necessary work).

Patch-ups

If a movie isn't working and the producer/studio/backers can't or don't want to spend the money to do any additional filming, then the director and editor have to find ways to solve the problems using the footage they have. Often this can lead to the use of efficient but clumsy devices such as explanatory crawls, title cards, or voice-over narration to clarify unclear (or nonexistent) story points or patch over the holes in poorly constructed plotlines.

More previews

The new and hopefully improved version of the movie may be previewed again so the filmmakers can see how well the changes work. Hopefully, the audience response is positive. If not, more changes may be made.

Ratings

When an American movie is near completion, it is shown to the Classifications & Ratings Administration (CARA), an independent agency that assigns ratings for all films produced by the Motion Picture Association of America. The MPAA is a trade organization whose members include all of the major studios and many of the independent film companies in the United States. The purpose of the MPAA rating system is to help parents decide what movies are appropriate for their children to see. The current ratings are:

- G: General Audiences—All Ages Admitted
- PG: Parental Guidance Suggested—Some Material May Not Be Suitable for Children
- PG-13: Parents Strongly Cautioned—Some Material May Be Inappropriate for Children Under 13
- R: Restricted—Under 17 Required Accompanying Parent of Adult Guardian
- NC-17: No One 17 and Under Admitted.

The more restrictive the rating, the narrower the film's potential audience is and the smaller its potential earnings.

Directors of independent films usually have wide latitude when it comes to what rating their pictures earn; they're usually made for relatively low budgets, so independent films don't have to appeal to a mass audience to earn their costs back, therefore a relatively restricted rating is okay. However, the movies made by the major studios (especially in this blockbuster-centric era) are usually very expensive and so need to attract as wide an audience as possible to turn a profit.

Therefore, the directors of big-budget studio movies (even those with final cut) are often contractually obligated to deliver a picture that can earn a specific rating, one that ensures the picture can attract the widest possible audience. Family-oriented films are usually required to earn a G or PG rating; medium-budget comedies, dramas, and action movies a PG, PG-13, or an R; and big-budget spectaculars a PG or a PG-13. No major studio will release a film with an NC-17 rating, primarily because no major theater chain will play NC-17 films. Independent films can be released with an NC-17 because they play mostly in smaller art-house cinemas, which generally don't have a problem with the rating (because their patrons usually don't).

If a film receives what the studio considers an unsatisfactory rating, the director is expected to appeal to CARA and attempt to get the agency to change its mind. Failing that, the director is required to make alterations in the movie—usually cutting down on the amount of sex, violence, or coarse language (the three primary areas of CARA concern)—so that it can earn it the desired rating.

Most directors will attempt to make the fewest changes possible (sometimes removing just a few frames here or there) to appease CARA without damaging the integrity of the film. (Directors have been known to deliberately insert material into their films that they know the agency will object to, which they will then offer to excise in the hope that the material they really want included will slip by unnoticed.) Sometimes CARA will demand more extensive changes, at which point the director either needs to comply or to persuade the studio to release the film with a more restrictive rating.

Locking the picture

Eventually, after all voluntary and involuntary changes have been made, the film is deemed complete and the picture is "locked"—meaning that editing is complete and that no more changes can be made to the visuals.

Possessory credit

As part of the finishing process, credits are added to the beginning and end of the film. All directors receive a "directed by" credit. Some directors also negotiate for a possessory credit—a separate title that further asserts their creative authorship of the movie. The most common possessory credit is "A (Director's Name) Film," although some helmers prefer "A Film by (Director's Name)." The "A Film by . . ." credit is a controversial one because many in the filmmaking community feel it minimizes the contributions of all of the other members of the creative team (and because it's pretentious).

Timing

The final stage of working with the visuals in a film is to time them—to adjust the colors in each shot and brighten or darken the images so that they are consistent through-out, and so that they accurately reflect the director's and the cinematographer's creative intent.

Timing used to be a photochemical procedure done in a film lab, but these days it is a mostly digital process. It is supervised mainly by the cinematographer, but the direc-tor is on hand to offer his input throughout and sign off on the final result.

Sound effects

Throughout the editing process, the sound designer puts together the film's sound effects—combining sounds re-corded on the set during production with new effects he and his team create in post. As with all other aspects of the film, the director supervises and approves the sound designer's work or asks for changes if he is dissatisfied.

ADR

Actors are often required to rerecord portions of their dia-logue—to replace tracks that were poorly recorded during production or to improve their vocal performances. Some-times they are also required to record brand-new lines—to clarify existing story points or incorporate new ones into the narrative. These new lines will sometimes be dubbed over shots of the actors speaking to replace old lines or be laid in over shots in which the actor cannot be seen speaking (over shots of the actor's back or of another character's face; over wide shots of the set or of a vehicle the character is riding in; and so on). This process is called Automated Dialogue Replacement or Additional Dialogue Recording, and the director is always present during this process to guide the actors' performances in the same way he guided them on the set during principal photography.

Scoring

As the picture nears completion, the director shows it to the composer. Most film composers prefer to see a movie they are going to score in as close to a finished state as possible—ideally the locked picture—because their music must match the images, action, rhythms, and tempo of the final film exactly.

Together, the director and composer will "spot" the picture—decide which sections should have music and which should not. The director will tell the composer his ideas about the music—what mood he wants it to create and how he wants it to enhance, underline, or provide a counterpoint to the images and action that appear on the screen.

During editing, most directors will create a temp track—an assemblage of preexisting music put together to serve as a temporary soundtrack for the various cuts of the movie to give a sense of the type of music a director wants in a film and the way he wants it to function. Composers generally do not want to hear temp tracks because they don't want them to influence the creative choices they make while composing their scores—which they, of course, want to be completely fresh and original. However, many a director will become quite attached to his temp and will directly or indirectly urge the composer to model the music he creates after it. This can create a lot of tension, so directors are urged to do their best not to fall in love with their temps.

After the film has been spotted, the composer will go off and write the score. At various points, he will audition his ideas for the director, who will give his input. When the score is finished, an orchestra will be assembled and the music recorded. It will then be turned over to a music editor, who will painstakingly match it to the completed film.

Mixing

When all the film's sound elements—dialogue, effects, and music—are ready, they are mixed together into a single unified soundtrack. This is a laborious process that can take many days and the director is there for all of it, indicating his preferences—to emphasize the dialogue in one scene; to soften certain sound effects in another; to allow the music to dominate in a third; and so on—from the beginning of the film to the end.

Prints

The final step in the postproduction process is to make prints of the film to distribute to theaters. For most of the past century, film prints were physical objects, but these days more and more prints are digital. No matter what the format, the director and his team check the prints to make sure they look and sound the way they are supposed to.

When postproduction is complete, the movie is finished and ready to be sent out into the world.

CHAPTER 9

The Director and the Film's Release

Premiere

A movie usually begins its release with a premiere, which the director usually attends. The film then goes into general release in anywhere from a few to a few thousand theaters.

Promotion

The release of a film is usually preceded and accompanied by a promotional campaign. This is a key element in any film production because it is the mechanism the filmmakers use to persuade people to come and see their movie. As part of the promotional campaign, the director will do print, radio, television, and Internet interviews. He might attend screenings at which he will do Q&As and participate in panel discussions. If he's well known enough, he might appear on talk shows.

Alternate versions

In addition to the release print, several alternate versions of a movie are also produced:

- Foreign releases—versions of the film dubbed into various languages and sometimes edited to meet the requirements of local censor boards.
- An airline edition—since both adults and kids are part of the audience on a plane, PG-13 and R-rated films are cut to remove objectionable material and sometimes redubbed to remove objectionable language.
- A television version—edited and redubbed to remove objectionable material, a TV iteration may also contain alternate takes of potentially offensive shots that do not contain the inappropriate material. The movie's running time might also be cut or padded (with shots and scenes deleted from the theatrical cut) so that it will be able to play in rigid network time slots.

These variations are usually prepared by the producer or the studio. Some directors have the right to approve any alternate versions of their films written into their contracts and can veto any changes they don't like. If a director does not have this right and doesn't care for the alterations, he has the option to remove his name from the film and use a pseudonym on the offending variation (welcome back, Alan Smithee).

DVD/Blu-ray

After a film's theatrical run concludes, it is released on home video on DVD or Blu-ray discs. For this release, the director may record an audio commentary track or participate in supplemental features (such as "making of" documentaries and behind-the-scenes featurettes). He may also select or approve the selection of any outtakes or deleted scenes featured on the disc. If the movie is also being issued in an extended version (sometimes identified—not always accurately—as a "director's cut"), the director will usually supervise the preparation of this longer edition.

Once a film has been released in all of its various incarnations, the helmer's formal involvement with it is over. However, a director's relationship with his movie never really ends. It becomes part of his professional and artistic oeuvre, and he may (depending on the terms of his contract) continue to derive income from it. If the movie is a success, the director may be offered more helming work because of it, and so the film can either start or further his career. If the movie becomes especially popular or well regarded, the director may be asked to speak about it—informally and in academic, professional, and cultural settings—for years to come. Decades later, he may become involved in restoring and preserving the film's physical elements and transferring them to new media so that the movie can continue to live on. So, while the director may no longer be making the film, he will forever be its maker.

CHAPTER 10

Directing in Other Modes

The primary focus of this book has been on directing the narrative feature film, because it is the most common type of movie. There are, of course, other kinds of films and, while the core task—to conceive and execute a specific vision—is always the same, there are some differences in how these types of movies are directed.

Short films

All the tasks involved in directing a narrative short are the same as those involved in directing a feature, except that the length of everything—the schedule, the script, and the film itself—is obviously much shorter (and the budget is much smaller).

Animation

For an animated short or feature, the director works with the actors during preproduction, which is when they record their voices for the film. And obviously there's no physical production—no sets or costumes (although there is set and costume design) or lights or special effects. Instead, the director spends the majority of his time supervising animators as they craft the film's shots using cells and animation stands or (more likely these days) with a computer.

Documentaries

Documentaries don't have screenplays or actors or sets. However, the director still must have a strong central concept and vision for the film he wants to make to bring focus to the reporting, to the interviews, and most important, to the editing process. Editing is really where a documentary is directed, as the helmer works with the editor to shape, illustrate, and explain the film's central thesis. The documentary director must have as keen a sense of narrative and drama as the helmer of a fictional feature if he is to transform his collection of facts, figures, and talking heads into a compelling and involving movie.

Experimental films

There is no one type of experimental film (by definition, each project is pretty much sui generis), but most tend to be not overly interested in narrative and are more focused on using abstract imagery and vignettes to provoke a reaction or to create an effect than in telling a story. Therefore, the directors of experimental films tend to concentrate more on the design, the photography, the editing, and the sound work, and less (if at all) on performance and dramaturgy.

Acknowledgments

I would like to thank Andrew Morton, Raymond J. Morton Sr. and M. F. Harmon for their input and assistance with this book.

Thanks to John Cerullo and Marybeth Keating at Hal Leonard for sparking this project. Thanks also to my agent, June Clark of FinePrint Literary Management, for her ongoing support and encouragement.

My deepest love to my family: Raymond J. Morton Sr. and Rita K. Morton; Kathy, Dan, and Caitlin Hoey; Nancy and John Bevacqua; Kate, Maddie, and Carrie Lutian; Rich and Kendra Morton; William Morton; Ken Morton; Claire, Derek, and Aiden James Masterbone; Andrew Morton; and Tom, Lindsey, Erin, Jack, and Sean Morton.

Love and appreciation also to my wonderful friends: Maggie Morrisette; M. F. and Linda Harmon; Carmen and Dan Apodaca; Terri Barbagallo; Dharmesh Chauhan; Jim DeFelice, Gina, David, Eva, and Hugo Fénard; Brian Finn, Faith Ginsberg; Tara, Kurt, Mia, and Mattius Johnson; Richard H. Kline; Michael Larobina, Alison, John, and Bethany

Aurora Nelson; Deborah McColl; Roger Nolan; Tim Partridge; Gary Pearle; Donna and Joe Romeo; David Shaw, Stephen Tropiano and Steven Ginsberg.

All my love to Ana Maria Apodaca, who is always front-row center.

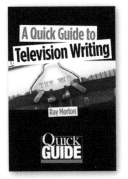

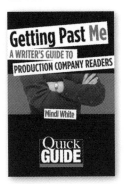